"*Positivity* QUOTES EMPOWERING INSIGHTS FOR *Daily Living*"

Elaine Fredrich

ISBN: 978-1-990543-20-3
Quotes arranged by K. Ruby Hopkins, Shayna Lewis
Cover and Interior Design by Ashley Russell Designs

Published by NextGen Story: Custom Publishing
www.nextgenstory.com

Dedicated to my
granddaughters

Author's Note

This book began as a set of quotes written in a notebook in my home – quotes that I came across which captivated me with their power and wisdom. I decided to compile them into a book for myself, my grandchildren, and my friends to help navigate life's ups and downs, providing comfort and guidance.

I believe these quotes hold the potential to uplift anyone who encounters them, offering inspiration during tough times. The anonymity of many quotes highlights their universal relevance—what matters most is the connection they create. I invite you to explore this collection, hoping that these words will provide the strength and guidance they have given me.

— *Elaine Fredrich, November 2024*

Contents

Self-Respect and Personal Growth

Integrity and Honesty

Romantic Love and Relationships

Loyalty

and

Trust

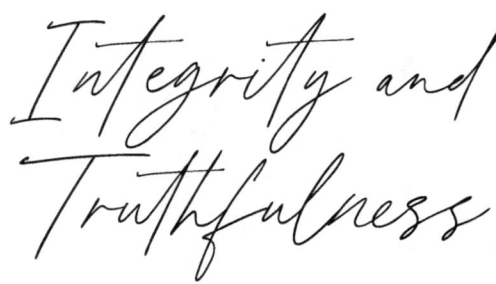

Integrity and Truthfulness

"People with good intentions make promises, but people with good character keep them."

— — — —

"Integrity is choosing your thoughts and actions based on values rather than personal gain."

— — — —

"It's not about who's nice to your face. It's about who stays loyal behind your back."

— — — —

"Never lie to someone who trusts you.
And never trust someone who lies to you."

— — — —

"Wrong is wrong, even if everyone is doing it.
Right is right, even if no one is doing it."

— — — —

"Respect is earned. Honesty is appreciated.
Trust is gained. Loyalty is returned."

— — — —

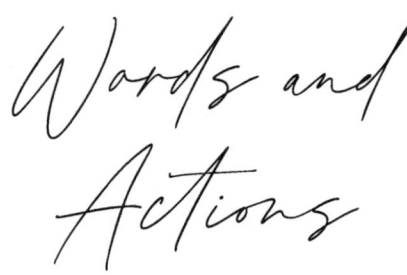

Words and Actions

"Loyalty is hard to find. Trust is easy to lose. Actions speak louder than words."

– – – – –

"Never trust words. Some people have sugar on their lips but venom in their hearts."

– – – – –

"Actions prove who someone is. Words just prove who they pretend to be."

– – – – –

"When you are important to another person, that person will always find a way to make time for you. No excuses, no lies, and no broken promises."

— — — —

"Anyone can give material things, but giving attention, loyalty, effort, and honesty is priceless."

— — — —

"Actions speak louder than words. Next time someone tries to convince you that they care, look at what they do, not what they say."

— — — —

"Love is nothing without actions. Trust is nothing without proof. Sorry is nothing without change."

— — — —

Harmful Behaviours and Broken Trust

"Three things you should never break: promises, trust, and someone's heart."

– – – –

"In a toxic family system, the black sheep is often just a person who sees through everyone else's manipulation."

– – – –

"Breaking someone's trust is like crumpling up a perfect piece of paper. You can smooth it over, but it's never going to be the same again."

– – – –

"Never misuse the one who likes you. Never say I'm busy to the one who needs you. Never cheat the one who really trusts you. Never forget the one who always remembers you."

— — — —

"Life has taught me that you can't control someone's loyalty. No matter how good you are to them, doesn't mean that they will treat you the same. No matter how much they mean to you, doesn't mean that they'll value you the same. Sometimes the people you love the most turn out to be the people you can trust the least."

— — — —

"Never argue with liars. You can't win, because they believe their own lies."

— — — —

"Stop expecting loyalty from people who can't even give you honesty."

－ － － －

"Never trust someone who has let you down more than two times. Once was a warning, twice was a lesson, and anything more than that is simply taking advantage."

－ － － －

"If you don't know the value of loyalty, you will never understand the damage of betrayal."

－ － － －

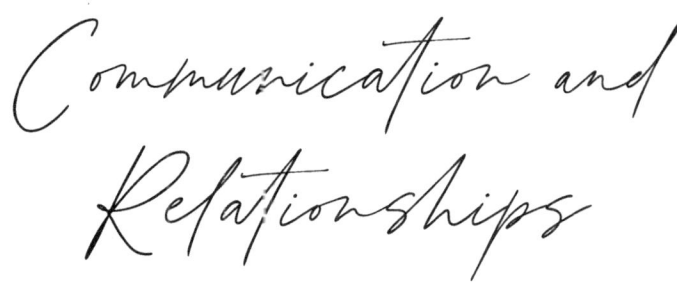

Communication and Relationships

"Trust is the building block of all relationships."

— — — —

"A true relationship is when you can tell each other anything, and everything. No secrets, no lies, only honesty."

— — — —

"Correct each other in private. Defend each other in public and keep your personal business off social media."

— — — —

"If you wanted me to speak more highly of you, then maybe you should have treated me better."

— — — —

"Without communication, there is no relationship. Without respect, there is no love. Without trust, there is no reason to continue."

— — — —

"Don't chase people. Be yourself, do your own thing, and work hard. The right people, the ones who really belong in your life, will come to you and stay."

— — — —

""Sorry" works when a mistake is made, but not when trust is broken. So in life, make mistakes but never break a trust. Because forgiving is easy, but forgetting and trusting again is sometimes impossible.**"**

— — — —

"One of the biggest lies ever told is "blood makes you family." No, that's NOT TRUE!! Blood makes you related; loyalty, love, and trust makes you family.**"**

— — — —

"Love is worth fighting for, but sometimes you can't be the only one fighting. At times, people need to fight for you! If they don't, find someone who is proud to have you, scared to lose you, fights for you, appreciates you, respects you, cares for you, and loves you unconditionally.**"**

— — — —

Respect

and

Boundaries

Respect

"Trust is earned, respect is given, and loyalty is demonstrated. The betrayal of any one of these is to lose all three."

— — — —

"Respect for ourselves guides our morals. Respect for others guides our manners."

— — — —

"Respect is one of the greatest expressions of love."

— — — —

"One of the most sincere forms of respect is actually listening to what another person has to say."

— — — —

"Before letting the words leave your lips, always consider how they will affect the other person. So much unnecessary pain is caused by words spoken in haste."

— — — —

"I admire women who are highly aware of their worth and are still so humble, kind, and supportive towards other women."

— — — —

"A man with manners and respect is a real definition of handsome."

— — — —

"Being classy is not about being stuck up, but more so about having a simply unique style that will never be forgotten. To be classy is to have respect, respect for others, respect for elders, and most of all respect for yourself."

— — — —

Disrespect

"You can't force someone to respect you, but you can refuse to be disrespected."

– – – –

"Life is too short to waste your time on people who don't respect, appreciate, and value you."

– – – –

"Don't let anyone get comfortable with disrespecting you. Your boundaries teach people how you should be treated."

– – – –

"There isn't a single person on this planet who is entitled to treat you badly. Remember that."

— — — —

"If you constantly have to tell someone the same exact thing about how you feel and they don't change it, understand they don't respect you."

— — — —

"Two things I don't like: a disrespectful child and a parent who thinks it's funny. Manners are very important."

— — — —

"To disagree with someone is not a bad thing. But it's not okay to disrespect, degrade, and humiliate that person."

— — — —

"There's a certain disrespect that an apology or explanation just doesn't fix."

— — — —

"The funny thing is, when you don't let people disrespect you, they start calling you difficult."

— — — —

"If someone treats you badly, just remember that there is something wrong with them, not you. Normal people don't go around destroying other human beings."

— — — —

Setting Boundaries

"You don't ever have to feel guilty about removing toxic people from your life. It doesn't matter whether someone is a relative, romantic interest, employer, childhood friend, or new acquaintance. You don't have to make room for people who cause you pain or make you feel small. It's one thing if a person owns up to their behaviour and makes an effort to change. But, if a person disregards your feelings, ignores your boundaries, and "continues" to treat you in a harmful way, let them go."

- - - -

"You have to learn to say no without feeling guilty. Setting boundaries is healthy. You need to learn to respect and take care of yourself."

— — — —

"A lack of boundaries invites a lack of respect. You are allowed to terminate toxic relationships. You are allowed to walk away from people who hurt you. You don't owe anyone an explanation for taking care of yourself."

— — — —

"Learn the art of saying no. Don't lie. Don't make excuses. Don't over-explain yourself. Just simply decline."

— — — —

Creating Distance

"Stay away from people who act like a victim in a problem they created."

"Distance is my new answer to disrespect. I no longer react. I no longer argue. I no longer dive into drama. I simply remove my presence. Peace of mind!"

"Distance yourself from the people who:
Lie to you
Disrespect you
Use you
Put you down
Drag you down"

— — — —

"Avoiding certain people to protect your emotional health is not weakness. It is wisdom."

— — — —

Walking Away and Letting Go

"Walking away can be an act of self-respect and courage. It's choosing your wellbeing over drama or toxic situations."

— — — —

"There are some people who always seem angry and continuously look for conflict. Walk away; the battle they are fighting isn't with you, it is with themselves."

— — — —

"Maturity is learning to walk away from people and situations that threaten your peace of mind, self-respect, values, morals, or self-worth."

— — — —

"If someone is continually toxic, cannot apologize, and always seems to blame others, let them go and make way for peace, calmness, and love in your life."

— — — —

"Sometimes you have to leave people behind. If they choose to take the right path, they will catch up. But, never go down the wrong path with them."

— — — —

"No matter how badly someone treats you, have the courage and wisdom to walk away. I know it's hard, but it's worse if you drop down to their level. Keep calm and stay strong."

— — — —

"Let go of relationships that do not serve you. That means negative people, dishonest people, people who don't respect you, people who are overly critical, and relationships that prevent you from growing. Prioritize connections that uplift, inspire, and empower you."

— — — —

"Cutting someone completely off from your life is sometimes necessary for your peace. Don't feel guilty about it."

— — — —

"Life becomes easier when you "delete" the negative people from it."

— — — —

Forgiveness and Second Chances

"Never go back to someone who chose someone else over you. Don't do that to yourself."

- - - -

"Apologies are meaningless when you continue to repeat the behaviour you are sorry for."

- - - -

"A toxic person never changes. They change victims and blame everything on everybody else."

— — — —

"I forgive, but I also learn a lesson. I won't hate you, but I'll never get close enough for you to hurt me again. I can't let my forgiveness become foolishness."

— — — —

"You can forgive some people without welcoming them back into your life. Apology accepted, <u>access denied</u>."

— — — —

Communication

"People who can't communicate think everything is an argument. And people who lack accountability think everything is an attack."

— — — —

"You had me with your words.
You lost me with your actions."

— — — —

"Lack of communication ruins everything because instead of knowing how the other person is feeling, we just assume."

— — — —

"Those who gossip to you will also gossip about you. Be mindful of the company you keep."

— — — —

"You should be able to tell a friend or a partner that they've upset you and then bounce back. But too many people don't know how to take accountability, and are quick to jump into defensive mode."

— — — —

Perception

"Perception can be confusing. People may say you hurt them, but what you might have done was say your truth, stood up for yourself, said no, protected your heart/energy, opted out, made an inner decision. Maybe they need a reminder about boundaries, entitlement, human rights."

— — — —

"There is nothing worse than people who only see things from their point of view and refuse to try to understand anything from someone else's perspective."

— — — —

"Never make someone a priority when all you are to them is an option."

— — — —

"You can't change someone who doesn't see an issue in their actions."

— — — —

Maintaining Relationships

"You don't need to maintain relationships with relatives who persistently try to undermine or harm you."

— — — —

"You are not obligated to have relationships with family members who are not good for your mental health."

— — — —

"Without respect, relationships are lost. We're all different and if someone can't value your differences and respect your values and beliefs, then they don't deserve a front row seat in your life."

— — — —

"You can't treat people like crap and then expect them to love you."

— — — —

"In a relationship you can't just do what you wanna do. You always have to consider how it will affect your partner. And that's what this generation doesn't understand."

— — — —

"Simple rule in life: If you wouldn't like it done to you, don't do it to others."

— — — —

"Love is not all you need. You need mutual respect. You need support. You need trust. You need boundaries. You need people to be there when it matters. You need space to grow and acceptance when you do. You need people to show their love in a way you can understand."

— — — —

"You shouldn't have to explain why you deserve to be spoken to with respect and treated with human decency. Do not allow anyone, even if it's someone you love, to talk down to you, hurt you, or strip you of who you are in order to gain power over you. That isn't love. And it isn't how you should ever be treated."

— — — —

"You can't force anyone to value, respect, understand, or support you, but, you can choose to spend your time around people who do."

— — — —

Self-Protection

"When someone is mean, don't listen. When someone ruse, walk away. When someone tries to put you down, stay firm. Don't let someone else's bad behaviour destroy your inner peace."

— — — —

"When someone in your life is not treating you right, no matter how much you love them, you've got to love yourself more and walk away."

— — — —

"Be strong enough to stand alone, smart enough to know when you need help, and brave enough to ask for it."

— — — —

"Be careful what you tolerate. You are teaching people how to treat you."

— — — —

"Two things to remember in life: take care of our thoughts when you are alone, and take care of your words when you are with people."

— — — —

"Give, but don't allow yourself to be used.
Love, but don't allow your heart to be abused.
Trust, but don't be naïve.
Listen, but don't lose your own voice."

— — — —

"Surround yourself with people who talk about visions and ideas, not other people."

— — — —

"Ignoring the red flags because you wanna see the good in people will cost you later."

— — — —

"Protect your dignity. Don't over-call or text someone who is intentionally ignoring you. Go where you are respected and loved."

— — — —

Friendships

and

Relationships

Qualities of Healthy Relationships

"A great relationship is about two things: first, appreciating the similarities, and second, respecting the differences."

— — — —

"People who care about you will show you in the way they talk to you, the way they listen to you, and what they're willing to do for you. In the same ways, those who don't care about you will also make it clear. Pay attention."

— — — —

"Some people are like unpaid therapy. They come, they shine, make us smile, and never ask for anything in return. Those are important people."

— — — —

"If someone is trying to be there for you, then by all means, let them. It is a blessing to have someone look after you. It is a beautiful thing to have someone who genuinely cares."

— — — —

Choosing Friends and Partners

"Time decides who you meet in life, your heart decides who you want in your life, and your behaviour decides who stays in your life."

– – – –

"Life is too short. Spend it with friends who make you laugh and feel loved."

– – – –

"Not everyone will appreciate what you do for them. You have to figure out who is worth your kindness and who is just taking advantage."

– – – –

"The only people who deserve to be in your life are the ones who treat you with love, kindness, and respect."

— — — —

"Always seek people who will add value to your life and bring out the best in you. And of course, be that person for others."

— — — —

"Surround yourself with people who are good for your soul."

— — — —

"Sit with people who protect your name in your absence."

— — — —

"Surround yourself with people who:
Empower you
Believe in you
Support you
Uplift you
Motivate you
Appreciate you"

– – – –

"Listen to the positive people in your life, and ignore those that doubt, judge, and are disrespectful. They are not worth your energy and attention."

– – – –

"Surround yourself with people that push you to do better. No drama, jealousy, or mess. Just higher goals, good vibes, and positive energy."

– – – –

Impact of Healthy Relationships

"Notice and appreciate the people you're with when you feel that you're at your best. They usually are kind, honest, and gentle souls."

"Some people make you feel better when you're around them. They are sunshine to your soul and medicine for your mind."

"You glow differently with good people in your life."

"Your quality of life improves dramatically when you surround yourself with good, intelligent, kind-heart, positive, loving people."

— — — —

"Soulmates aren't just lovers, they're friends too. Your soulmate naturally recognizes you, vibes with you, and aligns with you. They deeply understand you, value you, support you, love you, heal with you, and grow with you. They make you feel beautiful in your own skin just for being you."

— — — —

"The people in your life should be a source of reduction stress, not causing more of it."

— — — —

"In life, you will realize there is a role for everyone you meet. Some will test you. Some will use you. Some will love you and some will teach you. But the ones who are truly important are the ones who bring out the best in you. They are the rare and amazing people who remind you why it's worth it."

— — — —

Authenticity

"A true friend doesn't care if you're broke, upset, what you weigh, if your house is a mess, what car you drive, or if your family is filled with crazy people. They love you for who you are."

— — — —

"Never lose yourself while trying to hold onto someone who doesn't care about losing you."

— — — —

"Sensitive people should be treasured. They love deeply and think deeply about life. They are loyal, honest, and true. The simple things sometimes mean the most to them. They don't need to change or harden. Their purity makes them who they are."

— — — —

"It's important to make friendships that are deeper than gossiping, drinking, smoking, and going out. Make friends you can go get breakfast with. Make friends who support your life goals and believe in you."

— — — —

"Sometimes you just need a friend who will let you say your inner thoughts out loud without judgment or advice, so you can process how you're feeling."

— — — —

Commitment and Loyalty

"Family isn't always blood. It's the people in your life who want you in theirs. The ones who accept you for who you are. The ones who would do anything to see you smile, and love you no matter what."

– – – –

"People come and go in your life, but the right ones will stay."

– – – –

"Friendship isn't about who you've known the longest. It's about who walked into your life, said I'm here for you, and proved it."

– – – –

"Don't ignore the effort of a person who tries to keep in touch. It's not all the time someone cares."

— — — —

"True friends are the ones who lift you up when no one else has noticed you've fallen."

— — — —

"People who defend your name when you're not around, are the most loyal friends you could ever have."

— — — —

"When you really matter to someone, that person will always make time for you. No excuses, no lies, and no broken promises."

— — — —

"Once you love someone, you love them forever. People fall out of trust, intimacy, and respect, not love."

— — — —

"Never ignore a person who cares for you. Because someday you'll realize you've lost a diamond, while you were busy collecting stones."

— — — —

"When someone truly cares about you, they make an effort, not an excuse."

— — — —

Toxic Behaviours

"When people treat you like they don't care, believe them."

— — — —

"Never chase love, affection, or attention. If it can't be given freely by another person, it isn't worth having."

— — — —

"Sometimes people pretend you're a bad person so they don't feel guilty about the things they did to you."

— — — —

"Relationships don't work because people think it's okay to ignore somebody when they are mad, instead of being an adult and communicating."

— — — —

"Fake friends believe in rumours.
Real friends believe in you."

— — — —

"Two things you will never have to chase:
true friends and true love."

— — — —

"There will be people that would rather lose you than be honest about what they've done to you. Let them go!"

— — — —

"Don't waste another minute dealing with a toxic, negative, energy-draining person. Some people are wired for negativity. They love being argumentative, combative, and abusive. Run for your life as quickly as possible."

— — — —

"When people are rude to you, they reveal who they are, not who you are. Don't take it personally."

— — — —

"When other people treat you poorly, keep being you. Don't ever let someone else's bitterness change the person you are."

— — — —

Conflict Management

"Sometimes you gotta put aside what you feel for them, and pay attention to what their actions are saying, what they feel for you."

— — — —

"Little reminder: you are allowed to talk about what they did to you and how it hurt you. It does not matter how they feel about you talking about it, because if they wanted people to think better of them, they should have been better."

— — — —

Ending Relationships

"At some point, you must accept that some people can stay in your heart but not in your life."

— — — —

"We don't walk away to teach people a lesson. We walk away because we finally have learned ours."

— — — —

"Don't be afraid of losing someone who is not grateful to have you."

— — — —

"In life, we never lose friends. We only learn who the true ones are."

— — — —

Wisdom

and

Life Lessons

Choosing Our Mindset

"We are not given a good life or a bad life. We are given a life. It's up to us to make it good or bad."

– – – –

"If you focus on the hurt, you will continue to suffer. If you focus on the lesson, you will continue to grow."

– – – –

"The 3 Cs of life: choices, chances, changes. You must make the choice, to take a chance, if you want anything in life to change."

– – – –

"You either get bitter or you get better. It's that simple. You either take what has been dealt to you and allow it to make you a better person, or you allow it to tear you down. The choice does not belong to fate, it belongs to you."

– – – –

"A bad attitude can literally block love, blessings, and destiny from finding you. Don't be the reason you don't succeed."

– – – –

"A negative mind will never give you a positive life."

– – – –

"Life is about balance. Be kind, but don't let people abuse you. Trust, but don't be deceived. Be content, but never stop improving yourself."

– – – –

"Life is short. Cut out negativity, forget gossip, say goodbye to people who don't care. Spend time with people who are always there."

— — — —

"In my life, I've lived, I've loved, I've lost, I've missed, I've hurt, I've trusted, I've made mistakes, but most of all...I've learned."

— — — —

"Your mind is a powerful thing. When you fill it with positive thoughts, your life will begin to change."

— — — —

"Life humbles you. As you grow old, you stop chasing the big things and start valuing the little things. Alone time, enough sleep, a good diet, long walks, and quality time with loved ones. Simplicity becomes the ultimate goal."

— — — —

"5 harsh truths about life:
You are responsible for your own happiness.
The majority of your limits are self-imposed.
You can never fully prepare for everything life will
throw at you.
You will mess up. The best thing you can do is learn
from it and move on.
Your loved ones will not be around forever.
Cherish them."

— — — —

Controlling Our Words

"Sometimes silence makes a louder statement than saying anything at all."

– – – –

"Sometimes, not saying anything is the best answer. You see, silence can never be misquoted."

– – – –

"Once you are matured, you will realize that silence is more powerful than proving your point."

– – – –

"Two things to remember in life: "Take care of your thoughts when you are alone," and "take care of your words when you are with people.""

— — — —

"Never speak from a place of hate, jealousy, anger, or insecurity. Evaluate your words before you let them leave your lips. Sometimes it's best to be quiet."

— — — —

"3 things to keep private:
Your love life
Your income
Your next move"

— — — —

"Before you speak: THINK
T = Is it true?
H = Is it helpful?
I = Is it inspiring?
N = Is it necessary?
K = Is it kind?"

– – – –

"Sometimes quiet people really do have a lot to say…
They're just being careful about who they open up to."

– – – –

Making Mistakes

"A mistake that makes you humble, is better than an achievement that makes you arrogant."

— — — —

"If you make a mistake, apologize. If you are thankful, say it. If you are confused, ask questions. If you learn something, teach it. If you are stuck, ask for help. If you are wrong, admit it. If you can unselfishly give, give. If you love someone, tell them now."

— — — —

"The first to apologize is the bravest. The first to forgive is the strongest. And the first to forget is the happiest."

— — — —

"Don't carry your mistakes around with you. Instead, place them under your feet and use them as stepping stones to rise above them."

— — — —

"Everyone makes mistakes in life, but that doesn't mean they have to pay for them the rest of their life. Sometimes good people make bad choices. It doesn't mean they are bad. It means they are human."

— — — —

"A mistake repeated more than once is a choice."

— — — —

Staying Informed

"Before you assume, learn the facts. Before you judge, understand why. Before you hurt someone, "feel." Before you speak, think."

— — — —

"Don't be so quick to believe what you hear, because lies spread quicker than the truth."

— — — —

"Gossip dies when it hits a wise person's ears. Rumours
are started by haters, carried by fools,
and believed by idiots."

— — — —

"Just because I bring something up, it doesn't mean I
want to argue. I want to resolve things, get clarity, learn,
and grow together. We are adults—communicate."

— — — —

Sharing Wisdom

"Don't educate your children to be rich. Educate them to be happy, so they know <u>the value of things, not the price.</u>"

— — — —

"It's not what you do for your children, but what you have taught them to do for themselves that will makes them successful human beings."

— — — —

"I don't want my children to follow in my footsteps. I want them to take the path next to me and go further than I could have ever dreamt possible."

— — — —

"Strength grows when we dare, unity grows when we pair, love grows when we share, and relation grows when we care. Live in peace, not in pieces."

— — — —

"Whatever enters your children's eyes and ears enters their heart. Be careful of the things you say and do in their presence."

— — — —

Taking Action

"Life lessons: Give, but don't allow yourself to be used. Love, but don't allow your heart to be abused. Trust, but don't be naïve. Listen, but don't lose your voice."

— — — —

"Maybe I was raised wrong, but I was taught if you want something, you work for it!"

— — — —

"Knowledge is not powerful until it is used!"

— — — —

"Six ethics of life:
Before you speak—listen
Before you spend—earn
Before you quit—try
Before you write—think
Before you die—live
Before you rest—work"

— — — —

"I live by 3 simple rules:
Love needs action.
Trust needs proof.
Sorry needs change."

— — — —

"We make time for the things we love and excuses for
things we don't."

— — — —

Dealing with Difficult People

"You gotta understand that some people never really grow. They never learn their lesson. They never recognize their mistakes, they never acknowledge their faults, they never admit they were in the wrong. You will never receive an apology from them, and you will never see their behaviour change."

– – – –

"Narcissists always see themselves as victims no matter how horrible they've treated someone else. To them, the problem is not their lying, cheating, stealing, and abuse. The problem is that you started to notice those things."

— — — —

"Don't give them a taste of their own medicine. They already know what it tastes like. Give them a taste of your own medicine. If they lied, let your medicine be honesty! If they played with your emotions, let your medicine be maturity. Don't be afraid to be yourself, even if it means removing yourself from lives that you want to be in. You are, no doubt, worthy of being valued for who you are. So be who you are."

— — — —

"Some people could be given an entire field of roses and only see the thorns in it. Others could be given a single weed and only see the wildflower in it. Perception is a key component to gratitude, and gratitude is a key component to joy."

"The less you respond to negative people, the more peaceful your life becomes."

"Everything that irritates us about others can lead us to an understanding of ourselves."

Controlling Our Behaviour

"Don't let yourself be controlled by three things: people, money, or past experiences."

— — — —

"Every time you get upset at something, ask yourself if you were to die tomorrow, was it worth wasting your time being angry."

— — — —

"A meaningful life is not being rich, being popular, or being perfect. It's about being real, being humble, being able to share ourselves and touch the lives of others."

— — — —

"No matter how educated, talented, rich, or cool you believe you are, how you treat people ultimately tells all. Integrity is everything."

— — — —

"Love is nothing without action. Trust is nothing without proof. Sorry is nothing without change."

— — — —

"Your beliefs don't make you a better person. Your behaviour does."

— — — —

"Everything you do is based on the choices you make. It's not your parents, your past relationships, your job, the economy, the weather, an argument, or your age that is to blame. You and only you are responsible for every decision and choice you make. Period."

— — — —

"One of the best lessons you can learn in life is to master how to remain calm."

— — — —

"Learn how to:
Have fun without alcohol.
Talk without cellphones.
Love without conditions.
Dream without drugs.
Smile without selfies."

— — — —

"Practice the pause.
Pause before judging.
Pause before assuming.
Pause before accusing.
Pause whenever you're about to react harshly, and you'll
avoid doing any saying things you'll regret later."

— — — —

Responding to Hardship and Solving Problems

"Challenges make you responsible. Always remember that life without struggle is a life without success. Don't give up and learn "NOT TO QUIT."

- - - -

"Don't close the book. When bad things happen in your life, just turn the page and begin a new chapter."

- - - -

"There will be very painful moments in your life that will change you. Let them make you stronger, smarter, and kinder. But don't you go and become someone that you're not. Cry, scream if you have to. Then straighten out that crown and keep moving."

— — — —

"Be selective with your battles. Sometimes peace is better than being right."

— — — —

"We can't solve problems by using the same kind of thinking we used when we created them."

— — — —

"Most of the problems in life come because of two reasons: we act without thinking,and we keep thinking without acting."

– – – –

"10 awesome things money cannot buy:
Manners
Morals
Respect
Character
Common sense
Trust
Patience
Class
Integrity
Love"

– – – –

Discovering Someone's Character

"My psychology professor said: "When you fall in love with someone, you aren't interested in anyone else. If you are, you aren't in love," and I think everyone needs to hear that."

— — — —

"Time doesn't change people, time reveals the real face of people."

— — — —

"You cannot push anyone up a leader unless he be welling to climb a little himself."

— — — —

"Progress is impossible without change, and those who cannot change their minds cannot change anything."

— — — —

"Toxic people create chaos, point fingers, shift blame, and never take responsibility for their actions."

— — — —

"I don't wish bad upon nobody, but you reap what you sow in life. You don't treat people like shit and live a happy life."

— — — —

Positivity

and

Mental Strength

Happiness

"Happiness is a choice, not a result. Nothing will make
you happy until you choose to be happy. No person will
make you happy unless you decide to be happy.
Your happiness will not come to you.
It can only come from you."

– – – –

"Be happy. Be yourself. If others don't like it, then let
them be. Happiness is a choice. Life isn't about
pleasing everybody."

– – – –

"They key to being happy is knowing you have the power to choose what to accept and what to let go."

— — — —

"Happiness is the new rich. Inner peace is the new success. Health is the new wealth.
Kindness is the new cool."

— — — —

"The world would be a happier, more peaceful place if we all tried to understand instead of judging, paused before reacting, and gave each other the benefit of the doubt instead of assuming the worst."

— — — —

"Happy are those who take life day by day, complain very little, and are thankful for the little things in life."

– – – –

"Nothing good ever comes from ignoring your intuition. Trusting yourself can lead you to paths of greater clarity, growth, and happiness."

– – – –

Confidence

"Next time someone tries to bring you down, remember this: confidence is quiet, but insecurity is loud."

— — — —

"Always remember you are braver than you believe, stronger than you seem, smarter than you think, and loved more than you know."

— — — —

"Believing in yourself is the first secret to success."

— — — —

"You glow differently when your confidence is fueled by belief in yourself instead of validation from others."

━ ━ ━ ━

"Self-sabotage is the act of ruining exactly what you want because you subconsciously don't believe it's possible for you. When something great is happening in your life, embrace it fully and with an open heart. Disappointment hurts, but regret for not being our best can ache for a lifetime."

━ ━ ━ ━

"Start your day with a heart full of gratitude and a mind open to possibilities. Remember, each day is a new opportunity to make a positive impact and to grow stronger. Believe in yourself and your journey, and embrace the challenges as they come—they're just stepping stones to your success."

— — — —

Mental Training

"Train your mind to see the good in everything. Positivity is a choice. The happiness of your life depends on the quality of your thoughts."

– – – –

"When you can't control what's happening, challenge yourself to control the way you respond to what's happening. That's where your power is."

– – – –

"Your thoughts have immense power. Choose to fill your mind with positivity, gratitude, and self-belief. The way you think determines the way you experience life. Choose empowerment."

— — — —

"You don't dwell on disappointment. You've got to take the positives and keep looking ahead."

— — — —

"Train your mind to be stronger than your feelings."

— — — —

"Release whatever or whoever is causing you stress, heartache, unhappiness, uncertainty, or pain. It's time to shift."

"Your mind is a powerful thing. When you fill it with positive thoughts, your life will begin to change."

Emotional Regulation

"How you begin your day can make your day or break your day. Your attitude and actions have a strong effect on your whole day. Begin with a smile, a calmness of mind, and a heart filled with gratitude. A positive mindset that it's going to be a wonderful day."

— — — —

"Anger doesn't solve anything. It builds nothing, but it can destroy everything."

— — — —

"If you can stay positive in a negative situation, you win!"

— — — —

"No matter how you feel, get up, dress up, show up, and never give up."

— — — —

"When things feel overwhelming, remember one thought at a time, one taste at a time, one day at a time. Just breathe."

— — — —

"If you see someone is trying to make you angry or upset, do not react. It is not your job to make negative people happy."

— — — —

"If you get a gut feeling that something isn't right about someone or a situation, trust it."

— — — —

"You don't have to be positive all the time. It's perfectly okay to feel sad, angry, annoyed, frustrated, scared, or anxious. Having feelings doesn't make you a "negative person." It makes you human."

— — — —

"Sometimes you have to realize that the world is too beautiful to waste your time being angry or sad when you could be enjoying what life has to offer."

— — — —

"No matter what happens in life, keep a good heart. A heart of patience and trust. Don't let the darkness of this world harden your heart."

— — — —

Peace of Mind

"Peace of mind is important to maintain. Take care of
your thoughts. Take care of your feelings. Practice
gratitude. Make time for self-care. One of the best
lessons you can learn in life is to master
how to <u>remain calm</u>."

— — — —

"Health does not aways come from medicine. Most of
the time, it comes from peace of mind, peace in the
heart, peace in the soul. It comes from
laughter and love."

— — — —

"Peace of mind is a beautiful gift, which only we can give to ourselves just by expecting nothing from anyone."

— — — —

"Starting today, don't let situations or people drown out your inner peace. Surround yourself with positivity and uplift those around you. Remember, your mental health matters. Believe in yourself and watch amazing things happen."

— — — —

"At the end of the day, I'm at peace because my intentions are good and my heart is pure."

— — — —

Positive Influences

"You attract the energy that you give off. Spread good vibes. Think positively. Enjoy life."

- - - -

"Positivity isn't just a mindset, it's a way of life."

- - - -

"If you have someone in your life who is your home, your heart, your best friend, your safe space, then you are truly blessed beyond measure."

- - - -

"Surround yourself with positive people who will support you when it rains, not just when it shines."

– – – –

"Be careful what you hear about somebody. You might be hearing it from the problem."

– – – –

"Some people want material things. Me, I just want peace, happy times, and people that love me."

– – – –

Kindness

and

Compassion

Social Awareness

"Kindness begins with the understanding that we all struggle."

– – – –

"To be kind is more important than to be right. Many times, what people need is not a brilliant mind that speaks but a special heart that listens."

– – – –

"A smart person knows what to say. A nice person knows whether or not to say it."

– – – –

"People need to learn that their actions do affect other people. So be careful what you say and do, it's not always just about you."

— — — —

"People don't always need advice. Sometimes all they really need is a hand to hold, an ear to listen, and a heart to understand them."

— — — —

"Your smile is your logo, your personality is your business card, and the way you make others feel is your trademark."

— — — —

Honestly and Forgiveness

"Honesty without kindness is brutality, and kindness without honesty is manipulation."

— — — —

"Be there. Be open. Be honest. Be kind. Be willing to listen, understand, accept, support, and forgive. This is what it means to love."

— — — —

"Never apologize for being sensitive or emotional. It is a sign that you have a big heart, and that you aren't afraid to let others see it. Showing your emotions is a sign of strength."

— — — —

"Forgive others, not because they deserve forgiveness, but because you deserve peace."

— — — —

Children

"Raise your children to be impressed by kindness, loyalty, and humility, not just wealth, possessions, and power."

－ － － －

"Seven things every child needs to hear: I love you, I'm proud of you, I'm sorry, I forgive you, I'm listening, this is your responsibility, you have what it takes to succeed."

－ － － －

"When you keep criticizing your kids, they don't stop loving you. They stop loving themselves
Let that sink in."

— — — —

"Give your kids chores. Hold them accountable. Require honesty. Teach them respect. Raise your child. Don't just grow them."

— — — —

Real Beauty

"The most attractive thing about you should have less to do with your face or body and more to do with your heart and how you treat people."

— — — —

"A calm person is so attractive. Someone who doesn't resort to yelling or aggression in arguments. Someone who brings patience and peace."

— — — —

"A beautiful face will age and a perfect body will change, but a beautiful soul will always be a beautiful soul."

————

"I love people that have no idea how wonderful they are, and just wander around making the world a better place."

————

Measures of Strength and Success

"Strong people don't put others down, they lift them up."

— — — —

"When you love yourself, you glow from the inside. You attract people who love, respect, and appreciate your energy. Everything starts with how you feel about yourself. Start feeling worthy, valuable, and deserving of receiving the best life has to offer. Be magnetic."

— — — —

"Only people who are not happy with themselves are
mean to others. Remember that."

– – – –

"Be the reason why people believe in kindness, honesty,
integrity, and positivity."

– – – –

"Being rich has less to do with what you have in your
bank account, and more to do with what you
hold in your heart."

– – – –

"Life is not about being rich, being popular, or being
perfect. It's about being real, being humble,
and being kind."

– – – –

Acts of Kindness

"Being told you are appreciated is one of the simplest, most uplifting things you can hear."

— — — —

"When you love someone, you protect them from the pain. You don't become the cause of it."

— — — —

"Too often we underestimate the power of a touch, a smile, a kind word, a listening ear, an honest compliment, or the smallest act of caring, all of which have the potential to turn a life around."

— — — —

"It doesn't matter how dirty others play; karma has a big bite. Always move with a genuine heart and pure intentions."

— — — —

"Never play with the feelings of others. Because you may win the game, but lose the person forever."

— — — —

Self Respect

and

Personal Growth

Accountability

"I can respect any person who can put their ego aside and say, "I made a mistake. I apologize, and I'm correcting the behaviour."

— — — —

"You're not grown up until you know how to communicate, apologize, be truthful and accept accountability without blaming somebody else."

— — — —

"You must be big enough to admit your mistakes, smart enough to learn from them, and strong enough to correct them."

— — — —

"Mistakes are proof that you are trying."

— — — —

"Don't carry your mistakes around with you. Instead, place them under your feet and use them as stepping stones to rise above them."

— — — —

"Everything in your life is a reflection of a choice you have made. If you want a different result, make a different choice."

— — — —

"I choose to live by choice, not by chance. To makes changes, not excuses. To be motivated, not manipulated. To be useful, not used. To excel, not to compete. I choose self-esteem, not self-pity. I choose to listen to my inner voice, not the random opinion of others. I choose to be me."

— — — —

Discipline and Habit Formation

"Discipline leads to habits. Habits lead to consistency. Consistency leads to growth."

— — — —

"Self-discipline begins with the mastery of your thoughts. If you don't control what you think, you can't control what you do."

— — — —

"Actions prove who someone is, words just prove who they pretend to be."

— — — —

"Speed doesn't matter. Forward is forward. Little progress is progress, as long as you don't stop. You will get to the top. Just because you took longer than others, doesn't mean you failed."

— — — —

"Deep down you know exactly what you're capable of. There's even moments where you get a glimpse of all the potential you have. You can get there. You just have to be willing to sacrifice the habits, things, and situations that are standing in the way of your success."

— — — —

"Don't go back to less just because you are too impatient to wait for better."

— — — —

"Self-control makes the man. A man without discipline is a boy full of reactions, rather than a man of good actions."

— — — —

"Self-control is strength. Calmness is mastery. You have to get to a point where your mood doesn't shift based on the insignificant actions of someone else. Don't allow others to control the direction of your life. Don't allow your emotions to overpower your intelligence."

— — — —

"Success is not given. It is earned."

— — — —

"Three simple rules in life:
If you do not go after what you want,
you will never have it.
If you don't ask, the answer will always be NO.
If you do not step forward, you'll always be in
the same place."

— — — —

Strength of Character

"It is better to walk alone, than with a crowd going in the wrong direction."

– – – –

"Never lower your standards just because you are lonely. It is better to be by yourself than to be with the wrong person."

– – – –

"Once you've matured, you will realize that silence is more important than proving a point."

– – – –

"Strong women don't play victim, don't make themselves look pitiful, and don't point fingers. They stand and deal."

— — — —

"Be strong, but not rude. Be kind, but not weak. Be humble, but not shy. Be proud, but not arrogant."

— — — —

"Self-worth doesn't depend on the opinions of others; it is something you need to nurture from within."

— — — —

"If you carry one thing with you today, let it be this:
You are brave.
You are beautiful.
You are strong.
You are smart.
You are loved."

— — — —

"Love yourself enough to set boundaries. Your time and energy are precious. You get to choose how you use it. You teach people how to treat you by deciding what you will and won't accept."

— — — —

"Moving on doesn't mean forgetting. It means you choose happiness over hurt."

— — — —

Healthy Influences

"Choose to sit at the table where the talk is about growth, success, and goals, not about other people."

— — — —

"Never discredit your gut instinct. You are not paranoid. Your body can pick up on bad vibrations. If something deep inside of you says something is not right about a person or situation, trust it."

— — — —

"Get honest with people about who you are, what you want, and how you expect to be treated. Standards only scare off people who are not meant for you."

— — — —

"If money and material things make you believe you are better than others, you are the poorest person on earth."

— — — —

"You deserve people in your life who don't have misconceptions about your intentions or personality. You shouldn't have to constantly over-explain or defend yourself to those determined to find fault, especially when they are just projecting their own insecurities. Surround yourself with those who see the real you and love and appreciate you for who you truly are."

— — — —

"You don't need anyone's affection or approval in order to be good enough. When someone rejects or abandons or judges you, it isn't actually about you. It's about them and their own insecurities, limitations, and needs, and you don't have to internalize that. Your worth isn't contingent upon other people's acceptance of you—it's something inherent. You exist, and therefore you matter. You're allowed to voice your thoughts and feelings. You're allowed to assert your needs and take up space. You're allowed to hold onto the truth that who you are is exactly enough. And you're allowed to remove anyone from your life who makes you feel otherwise."

— — — —

Releasing Pain

"I have decided to stop saying yes to people and situations that don't support my wellbeing. Instead, I will say yes to my happiness, and yes to my growth, and yes to all the people and things that inspire me to be authentic and whole, while at the same time accepting me just as I am. My yes from here on out is my pledge to live honestly, my commitment to love myself fiercely, and my cry to create my best life possible. YES!"

- - - -

"It isn't your job to keep the peace of those who have caused chaos in your life. Your only job is to protect your own peace and happiness at whatever cost."

— — — —

"Not to spoil the ending for you, but you end up letting go of the pain and stress you're going through. You heal, you glow up, and you become more gorgeous, abundant, successful, and happy than you have ever been."

— — — —

Integrity
and
Honesty

Real Value

"There are four very important words in life: love, honesty, truth, respect. Without these in life, you have nothing."

— — — —

"Yes, I overthink, but not because I want to be sad. I just feel too much. I value things, emotions, people, and promises."

— — — —

"The truth doesn't cost anything, but a lie could cost you everything."

— — — —

"A single lie discovered is enough to create doubt in every truth expressed."

— — — —

"No matter how educated, talented, rich, or cool you believe you are, how you treat people ultimately tells all. Integrity is everything."

— — — —

"Money doesn't make a man. Muscles don't make a man. Tattoos don't make a man. Character is what makes a man! Let a man's character be his currency; that will tell you what he's really worth."

— — — —

"I'm not impressed by money, social status, or job title. I'm impressed by the way someone treats other human beings."

— — — —

"Honesty is the highest form of intimacy."

— — — —

"The greatness of a man is not in how much wealth he acquires, but in his integrity and his ability to affect those around him positively."

— — — —

Discernment

"A smart person knows what to say and is smart enough to know when to say nothing."

— — — —

"Before you speak, let your words pass through three gates: It is true? Is it necessary? Is it kind?"

— — — —

"If it is not right, do not do it.
If it is not true, do not say it."

— — — —

"Integrity is choosing your thoughts and actions based on values rather than personal gain."

— — — —

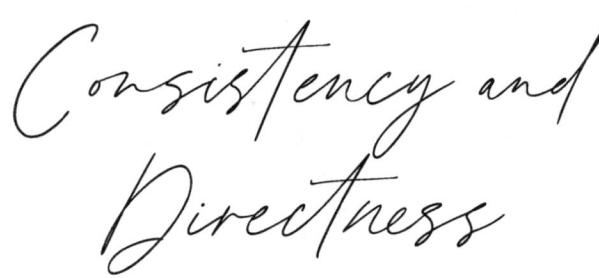

Consistency and Directness

"Do not be fooled!! A person's most consistent behaviour is their true self. "Period."

– – – –

"A real man will be honest no matter how painful the truth is. A coward hides behind lies and deceit."

– – – –

"I love real people who say what they mean and mean what they say. No fluff, no lies, and no pretense."

– – – –

"Unpopular fact: How someone treats you is how they feel about you. Don't try to decode it or make excuses for it. It's simple. If they act like they don't care, they don't care, because if they truly liked you and valued you, they would never put you in a position to question the way they act towards you, despite claims they love you. They'd just act right and show you what you're truly worth."

— — — —

"I respect those who tell the "truth," no matter how hard it is. Integrity is everything."

— — — —

"If you tell the truth, you don't have to remember anything."

— — — —

"I have a lot of respect for genuine people. They might not be perfect, but at least they are not pretending to be."

— — — —

"If you want to be trusted, be honest."

— — — —

Manipulation

"Sometimes you don't need to hear their excuses or what they have to say for themselves, because their actions already spoke the truth."

— — — —

"Someone who lacks accountability and instead blames you instead of correcting their own actions is trying to manipulate you."

— — — —

"An apology without change is just manipulation."

— — — —

"You're not grown until you know how to communicate, apologize, be truthful, and accept accountability without blaming someone else."

— — — —

"Never argue with someone who believes their own lies."

— — — —

"The audacity of how people blame you for how you reacted, but they never recognized what they did to make you react that way."

— — — —

"No matter how badly someone treats you, never drop down to their level. Remain calm, stay strong, and walk away."

— — — —

"Men are supposed to love and protect women, not to hurt and betray them."

— — — —

"Don't lie to me. I can respect a bad decision, but I can't respect a liar."

— — — —

Growth

"Facing your mistakes head-on isn't a sign of weakness; it's a display of strength and maturity. By righting your wrongs, you're not just repairing what's been broken, you're elevating your character and cultivating a sense of integrity."

– – – –

"Don't burn bridges. Keep your integrity. If you don't get along, just keep your distance."

– – – –

"Hurting them back isn't going to make you feel any better, and it isn't going to resolve anything. It will just make things harder. Please remember, revenge is never the answer. It just isn't, no matter how much they've hurt you. You're so much better than that."

– – – –

"The world is full of good people. If you cannot find one, be one."

– – – –

Romantic Love

and

Relationships

Singleness

"Stop looking for a partner. Focus on your goals and rebuilding your life. The right person will eventually find their way to you."

— — — —

"Don't be desperate. It's better to be single than to be taken for granted. Don't settle just because you're tired of waiting."

— — — —

"Being alone may scare you, but staying in a bad relationship will damage you."

— — — —

"Being with no one is better than being with the wrong one. Sometimes, those who fly solo have the strongest wings."

— — — —

A Noble Man

"A man who wants to make a relationship work will move mountains to keep the woman he loves."

— — — —

"Every woman deserves a man who calls her baby, kisses her like he means it, holds her like he never wants to let her go, doesn't cheat or lie, wipes her tears when she cries, doesn't make her jealous of other women, is not scared to let his friends know how he really feels about her, and lets her know how much he really loves her."

— — — —

"A real man will cut off any female that truly threatens his relationship with his woman."

————

"Winning a woman's heart doesn't make someone a man. Learning to treasure that heart after it's won is what makes someone a real man."

————

"If a man is in love with you:
He will apologize
He will sacrifice for you
He will be consistent
He will be loyal to you
He will defend you
He doesn't intentionally hurt you"

————

"So many men think women want money, cars, and gifts. But the right woman wants a man's time, effort, passion, honesty, loyalty, smile, and him choosing to put her as his priority."

— — — —

"Any man can treat a lady right for one night, but it takes a great man to treat her right for the rest of her life."

— — — —

"A real man understands that sex isn't everything when it comes to satisfying a lady, comforting her, appreciating her, respecting her...and taking care of her emotionally is also part of pleasing her."

— — — —

"One day you're going to come across a man that will worship the ground you walk on. Do not stop until you find that man. He will love you and cherish every inch of you (personality, body, mind, etc.). And he will do everything in his power not to lose you.
Don't settle for half the man."

– – – –

What to Look For in a Partner

"Don't go for looks, go for maturity, loyalty, honesty, and peace."

— — — —

"Invest your time in someone that makes you feel appreciated, even on your worst days.
That's real love."

— — — —

"Never get too attached to anyone unless they feel the same towards you, because one-sided expectations can mentally destroy you."

— — — —

"We think we want sex. It's not always about sex. It's intimacy we want. That's what we crave. To be touched. Looked at. Admired. Smiled at. Laugh with someone. Feel safe. Feel like someone's really got you."

— — — —

"Don't choose someone just because they're okay with being with you. Choose someone who's genuinely excited and eager to share their life with you. Someone real. Someone who wants to be there. Every day. Together."

— — — —

"I believe once you find your person, no one even interests you anymore. No one has the same vibe, no one matches your energy as much as they do. Everything is just with them. And not just relationship-wise, friendships as well."

— — — —

"I could talk to you for hours and not get tired of our voice or your laugh. I could never get tired of seeing your smile. I really could never get tired of you at all."

— — — —

"Be with someone who is proud of you, someone you can laugh with, someone who listens to you, understands you, who treats you well and makes you a priority."

— — — —

"Be with someone who loves you loudly, publicly, privately, and behind your back."

— — — —

"Find someone who is proud to have you, scared to lose you, fights for you, appreciates you, respects you, cares for you, and loves you unconditionally."

— — — —

"Many people will want you, but not want to love. There is a difference between wanting you and wanting to love you. Choose to be loved and not to be used."

— — — —

Making it Official

"What is the difference between I like you and I love you? Beautifully answered by Buddha: When you like a flower you just pluck it. But when you love a flower, you water it daily. One who understands this, understands life."

- - - -

"Fall in love with someone who deserves your heart, not someone who plays with it."

- - - -

"Fall in love with someone w ho wants you, who waits for you, and understands you even in the madness; someone who helps you, guides you, and someone who is your support, and your hope. Fall in love with someone who talks with you after a fight."

— — — —

"Your relationship doesn't need to make sense to anyone, except you and your partner. It's a relationship, not a community project."

— — — —

Forming Healthy Habits

"3 rules for a lasting relationship:
Never make your partner feel unwanted.
No matter how hard things get, never cheat.
Always have your partner's back through the good
and the bad times."

— — — —

"Without communication there's no relationship.
Without respect there is no love. Without trust there is
no reason to continue."

— — — —

"Be with someone that says,
"let's fix this. I can't lose you.""

— — — —

"Couples in a healthy relationship also argue, have
different opinions, feel frustrated, insecure, and bored
at time. Healthy doesn't mean perfect. What makes a
relationship perfect is how you choose to move through
those challenges together."

— — — —

"In a relationship you don't lie and keep secrets. You're
in a relationship to grow closer, not hide things
and ruin trust."

— — — —

Mutual Respect

"A relationship can only work between two people who are totally present and dedicated to one another, despite any outward distractions or internal problems. You're either in it together, or you're not in it at all."

— — — —

"Great relationships aren't great because they have no problems. They're great because both people care enough about each other to make it work."

— — — —

"A relationship means that you come together to make each other better. Believe in each other. Support each other. Build each other. Be their peace, not their problem."

— — — —

"Be with someone who motivates you to do better in life because relationships are more than just falling in love. It's about inspiring each other to become better versions of yourselves day in and day out."

— — — —

Breakups

"People don't leave relationships because the other person made a mistake. They usually leave because the mistake became a habit."

- - - -

"Breakups are OK. Starting over is okay. Moving on is OK. Saying no is OK. Being alone is OK. What is not okay is staying somewhere where you are not happy, valued, or appreciated."

- - - -

"Never leave a true relationship for a few faults. Nobody is perfect, and in the end, affection is always greater than perfection."

- - - -

Commitment and Marriage

"I do not want someone who stands next to me because they are lonely. I want someone who stands next to me because they can't imagine standing next to anyone else."

— — — —

"If someone seriously wants to be part of your life, they will seriously make an effort to be in it. No reasons. No excuses."

— — — —

"Don't believe those who tell you they love you. Believe those who show you they do."

— — — —

"A person becomes ten times more attractive, not by their looks but by their acts of kindness, respect, and honesty, and the loyalty they show."

– – – –

"Choose me or lose me. I'm not a backup plan and definitely not a second choice."

– – – –

"Someone who loves you wouldn't put themselves in a position to lose you."

– – – –

"Once in your life, you'll come across a special person that makes you happy, supports you, and makes you a better person. Don't let them go."

– – – –

"Marriage is not a guarantee for a happy life.
Marriage is either a beautiful commitment, or a long-term punishment. It takes two to sail a married life.
It takes understanding and trust. Not just love.
It takes a genuine friendship and not just intimacy.
And when the relationship is put to test,
it takes two willing souls to save it."

– – – –

"There are no perfect husbands and no perfect wives, but if you will keep believing in each other, there will be plenty of perfect moments in your marriage."

– – – –

True Love

"Love is just a word until someone comes along and gives it meaning."

— — — —

"Love is a combination of care, commitment, knowledge, responsibility, respect, and trust."

— — — —

"Real love is not based on romance, candle-lit dinners, and long walks on the beach. It is based on respect, compromise, care, and trust."

— — — —

"When love is real, it doesn't lie, cheat, pretend, hurt you, or make you feel unwanted."

— — — —

"You deserve a love that won't keep you up worrying. You deserve a love that feels like home. A love that is certain. A love that makes sense."

— — — —

"A good relationship is with someone who knows all your insecurities and imperfections but still loves you for who you are."

— — — —

"The perfect partner doesn't mean they buy you gifts 24/7, drives you around, or pays for everything. It means they don't let you go to bed upset, listen to you, treat you with respect, pay attention to you when you talk, and holds you, gives you priority no matter how busy they are."

— — — —

"True love is about growing as a couple, learning about each other, and never giving up on each other."

— — — —

End Note

"Sensitive people should be treasured.
They love deeply and think deeply about life.
They are loyal, honest, and true.
The simple things sometimes mean the most to them.
They don't need to change or harden.
Their purity makes them who they are."

I hope this book has enlightened you as much as it has
me in my daily life.

— *Elaine Fredrich*